Contents

HOUGHTON MIFFLIN SOCIAL STUDIES

To the Teacher ii

UNIT 1: PEOPLE EVERYWHERE
Unit Planner 1
Long-Term Project
Make a Community Mural Map 2
Geography Activities
Draw a Map 4
Use a Map Key 5
Hands-On Activity
Class Cube 6
Performance Activities
Fingerplay 8
Song 10

UNIT 2: WHERE WE LIVE
Unit Planner 13
Long-Term Project
Earth Book 14
Geography Activity
The Bear Went Over the Landforms 16
Hands-On Activities
Four-Seasons Circle 18
Natural Resource Bracelet 19
Performance Activities
Citizenship Cheer 20
Prop Talk Plan 22

UNIT 3: WORLD OF WORK
Unit Planner 25
Long-Term Project
Create a Class Store 26
Geography Activities
Goods and Services Map 28
Plan Places For New Services 29
Hands-On Activities
Better Butter Factory 30
Butter Booklet 31
Performance Activities
Chalk Talk 32
Choral Reading 34

UNIT 4: EVERYTHING CHANGES
Unit Planner 37
Long-Term Project
Create an Exhibit 38
Geography Activities
Make a Map 40
Transportation Graph 41
Hands-On Activities
Personal History Timeline 42
Make a Toss-and-Catch Game 43
Performance Activities
Pilgrim Talk 44
The Lost Mouser 46

UNIT 5: GOOD CITIZENS
Unit Planner 49
Long-Term Project
City and State Class Book 50
Geography Activity
Laws and Signs 52
Hands-On Activities
Make an Award Ribbon 54
U.S.A. Symbol Pop-up 55
Performance Activities
Meet a Hero or Leader 56
Lion for Mayor! Mouse for Mayor! 57
Personal Finance 60

CALENDAR ACTIVITIES
Calendar 70
January and February 71
March and April 72
May and June 73
July and August 74
September and October 75
November and December 76

Answer Key 77

To the Teacher

To many elementary teachers, social studies is the "dessert" of their teaching day: a subject that allows for interactive lessons and hands-on activities. It is also a subject for which there is usually little time in the course of the school day. Many teachers nevertheless find ways to incorporate projects, activities, simulations, and other performance activities into the classroom, to "bring social studies alive" for the children.

Activities in *Houghton Mifflin Social Studies*

Numerous sources exist for projects and activities, but the challenge for most teachers is to find options that are manageable, flexible, and support the required curriculum. *Houghton Mifflin Social Studies* addresses these concerns with activities that are

- **Realistic** Program activities use easy-to-find materials and span time blocks that can be easily scheduled.

- **Optional** Activities and projects engage and motivate children, yet are not required to cover the curriculum.

- **Based on tested objectives** Activities and projects are focused on required content and skills and use a hands-on, interactive approach to helping children learn the material they need to know.

These activities and projects are found in the following program components:

Student Book

- Hands-on and writing activities in each Lesson Review support different learning modalities and writing modes.

- Extend Lesson activities are leveled for extra support or challenge opportunities.

- Chapter Review activities synthesize important concepts of the chapter.

- Unit Reviews include opportunity for hands-on review and a Current Events project tied to information on the Web from Weekly Reader.

Bringing Social Studies Alive
ii   **Use with *School and Family***

Teacher's Edition

- Activities and projects in the Student Book are supported by scoring rubrics.

- Every unit begins with leveled and cross-curricular activities.

- Support for every Core Lesson includes activity suggestions for differentiated instruction and cross-curricular links.

- Extend Lesson support includes suggestions for activities for differentiated instruction and cross-curricular links.

Using *Bringing Social Studies Alive*

This booklet is organized to provide a variety of interactive activities and projects that are easily organized and managed. The Unit Planner illustrates the numerous topics covered in all the strands of social studies that include: Citizenship, Culture, Economics, Geography, and History. The planner also shows the instructional approaches used within each activity and an estimate of the time needed to complete it. For each unit you will find these opportunities:

- **Long-term Project** These projects develop over the course of the unit, to help children creatively synthesize large concepts and develop their writing, research, and presentation skills. In-depth support is provided for directing these projects.

- **Hands-on Activities** Shorter term and more focused than the projects, these activities cover different social studies subject areas in a variety of engaging ways.

- **Geography Activities** These activities cover map and globe skills and geography concepts to further develop geographic literacy.

- **Performance Activities** Citizenship simulations, Readers' Theater dramas, and other speaking and listening opportunities are included in these activities.

Bringing Social Studies Alive also features two special activity selections. These selections include:

- **Calendar Activities** Information on important dates and ideas for using the calendar are included to teach social studies concepts and skills.

- **Personal Finance Activities** These activities develop economic understanding through the personal finance skills children will need throughout their lives.

Use with *School and Family*

Unit Planner

	Materials Needed
Long-Term Project Pages 2–3	
Make a Community Mural Map Children make a map of their community. **Time Needed:** 4 weeks **Strand:** Culture **Lesson Link:** Lessons 2 and 4	• map of your community • butcher paper and tape • markers • crayons or colored pencils • construction paper • scissors
Geography Activities Pages 4–5	
Activity 1 **Draw a Map** Children draw a map of the school library. **Time Needed:** 20–30 minutes **Strand:** Geography **Lesson Link:** Lesson 2	none
Activity 2 **Use a Map Key** Children use a map key to answer questions about a map of a playground. **Time Needed:** 20–30 minutes **Strand:** Geography **Lesson Link:** Lesson 3	none
Hands-On Activities Pages 6–7	
Activity 1 **Class Cube** Children make a class cube of things that they do at school. **Time Needed:** 20–30 minutes **Strand:** Culture **Lesson Link:** Lesson 2	• scissors • crayons • tape
Activity 2 **Hand Puppets** Children make puppets for a play about working together. **Time Needed:** 20–30 minutes **Strand:** Culture **Lesson Link:** Lessons 1 and 2	• construction paper • crayons • craft materials such as yarn, pom-poms, or cloth scraps • glue
Performance Activities Pages 8–11	
Activity 1 **Fingerplay** The class puts on a fingerplay about working together. **Time Needed:** 20 minutes **Strand:** Economics **Lesson Link:** Lesson 2	none
Activity 2 **Song** Children write and sing a song about community helpers. **Time Needed:** 20 minutes **Strand:** Economics **Lesson Link:** Lesson 4	none
For Personal Finance, see pp. 60–69; for Calendar Activities, see pp. 70–76.	

1

Make a Community Mural Map

Introduction

In this activity, children work in small groups to make a mural map of their community. The project takes four weeks to complete. You may follow the plan below to organize the project.

Project Plan

Week 1: Discuss Community Places 30 minutes

Explain to children that they will be working together to make a map—a drawing of a place. Point out that their map will be large. It will cover one wall of the classroom. Tell children that the map will show places in your community.

Lead children in a discussion about important places in your community. Ask children to brainstorm important places in your city or town. Record children's responses.

Places in a Community

- schools
- libraries
- playgrounds
- business centers
- shopping centers
- airport

- bus station
- train station
- fire station
- police station
- hospitals
- homes

To prompt children in listing places in your community, you may ask the following questions:

- Where do people live?
- Where do people who help others work?
- Where are some other places that people work?
- Where do people visit for fun?
- Where do people shop?

Show children a map of your community. Help them locate on the map places they identified in the discussion. Tell children that they will include some of these places in their map of the community.

Week 2: Draw Roads 30 minutes

Tape the butcher paper to the wall where the map will be displayed. Use a marker to outline the general shape of your community. Display the printed community map, and point out major roads in the community. Have children label the roads on the map. Lead children in a discussion about the importance of the roads, and how they allow people to get from place to place. Organize children into small groups, and give each group a slip of paper with the name of a major road. Work with each small group to help them locate the road on the printed map. Have children first use pencil to draw their road on their map, allowing them to erase if necessary. Then have them go over their drawing with crayon or marker and label the road.

Week 3: Draw Buildings 40 minutes

Have children make a list of places in their community they want to include on their map. Choose one building and model drawing it and cutting it out to give children a sense of the scale of the map. Assign several buildings to each small group. Have children draw the buildings, cut them out, and label them.

Week 4: Complete the Map 60 minutes

Invite children to complete the map by attaching their cutouts to the map. Provide assistance as necessary about where each building should go, referring to the printed community map as needed. As group members attach each cutout, encourage them to talk about the importance of each place in their community. After the map is complete, you may invite school workers or another class to view it. The guests can ask children questions about it.

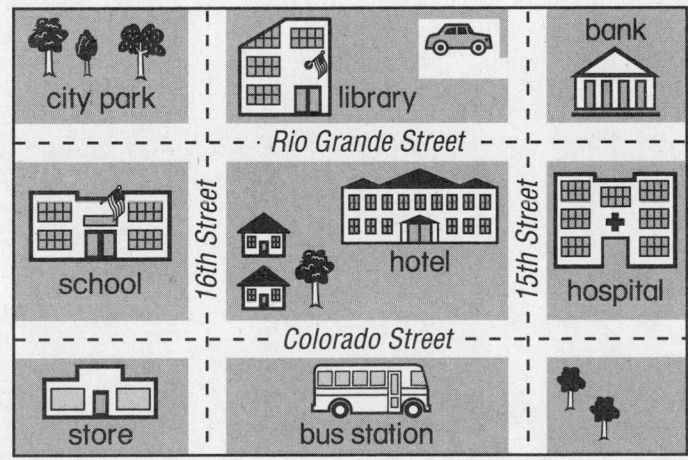

Name _____ Date _____

Draw a Map

This picture shows how a school library
looks from above.

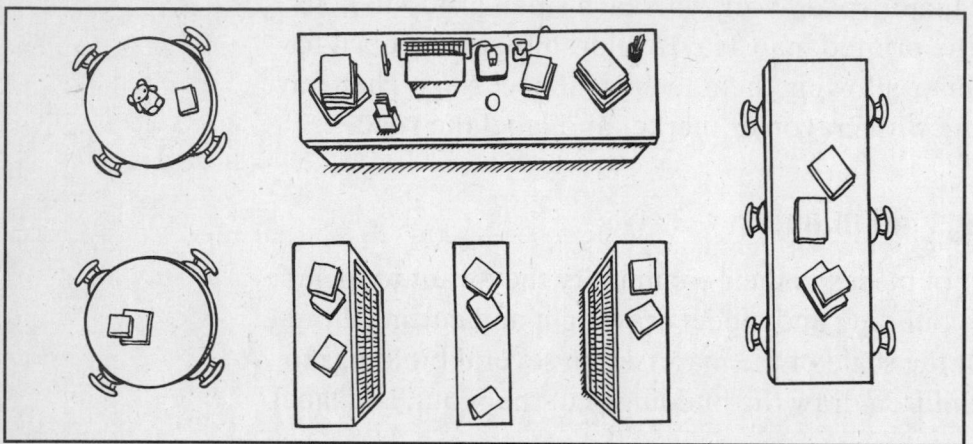

Name two things you see in this picture.

_____   _____

Draw a map of your library. Show how it looks
from above.

Name _____ Date _____

 # Use a Map Key

This map shows a playground.

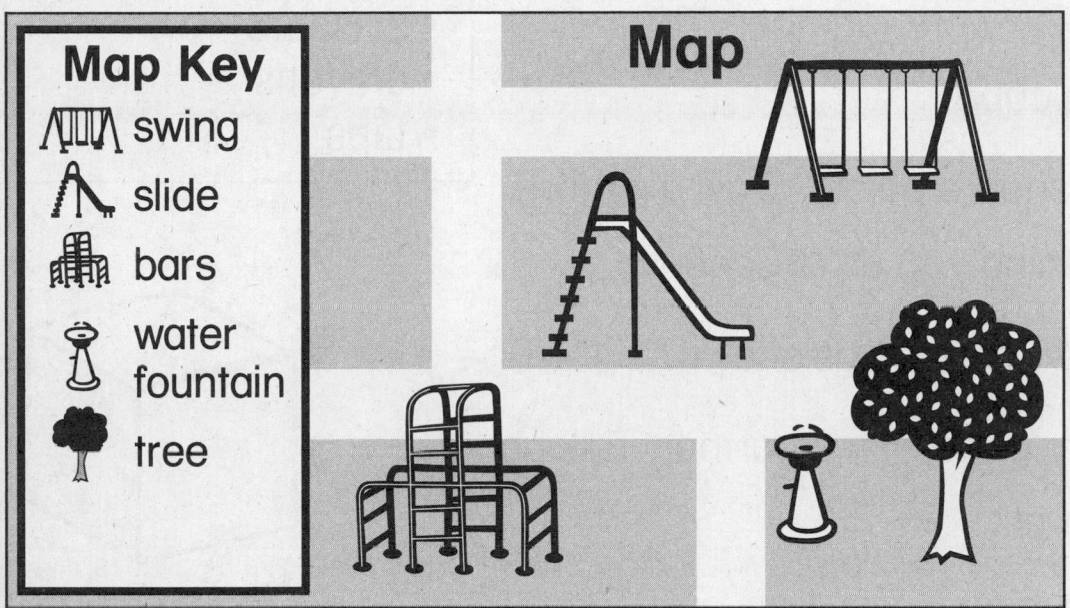

Map Key

swing	
slide	
bars	
water fountain	
tree	

Map

Use the map key to answer these questions about the map.

1. What does ⨳ stand for?

_____

2. What is the closest thing to the water fountain?

_____

3. What is between the swing and the bars?

_____

Bringing Social Studies Alive

Use with *School and Family*, Unit 1

Name _____ Date _____

Class Cube

Think about jobs you do at school. Think about ways you work together. Then make a class cube.

MATERIALS
- scissors
- crayons
- tape

1. In each square below, draw a picture of something you do at school.

2. Cut, fold, and tape as shown.

3. Toss your cube with a partner. Talk about the pictures.

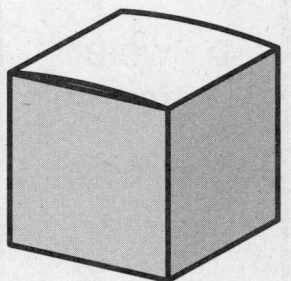

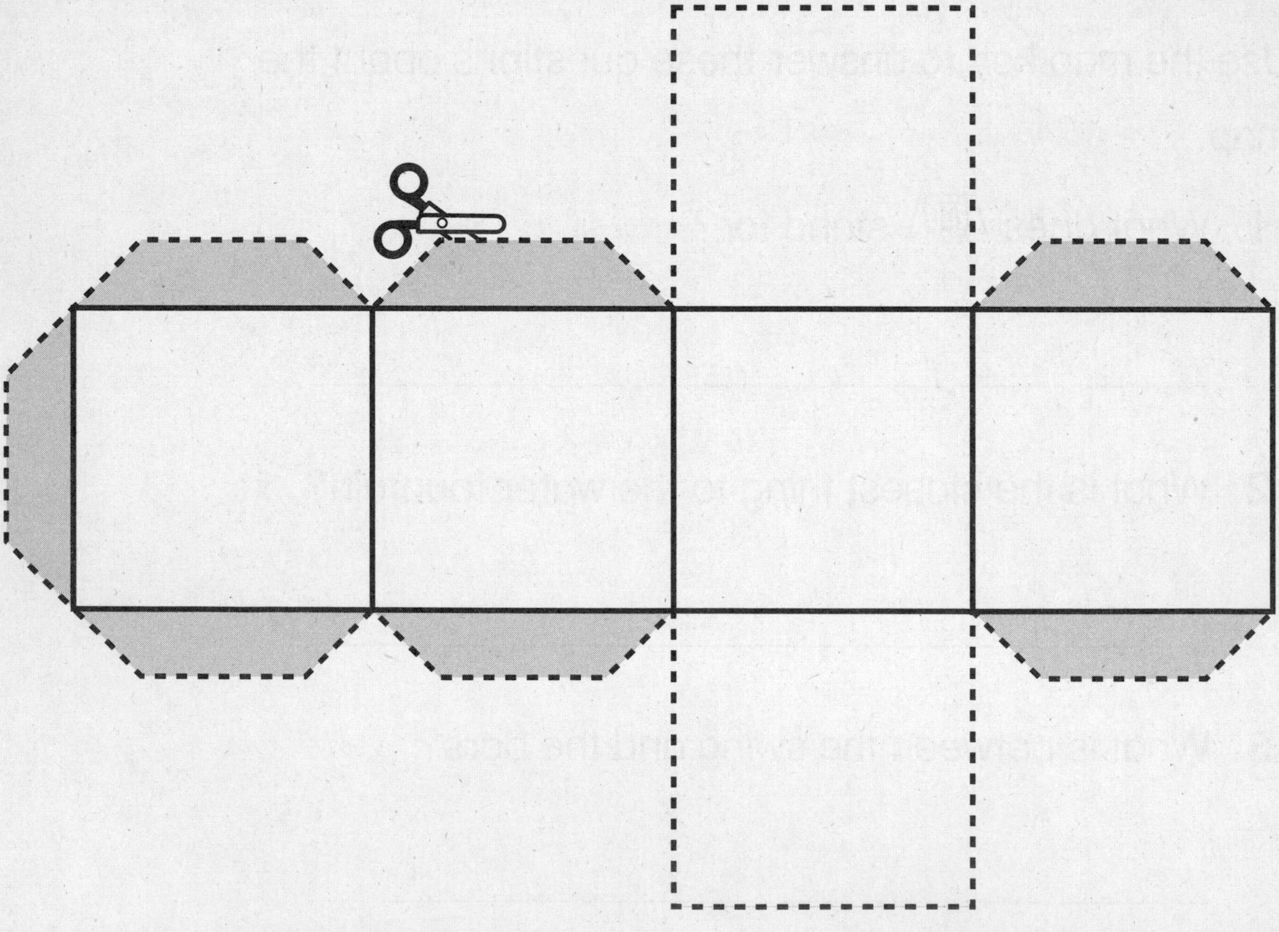

Name _____ Date _____

 **Hand Puppets**

Make two hand puppets. The puppets can be two people in a family or two people in a classroom.

MATERIALS
- construction paper
- crayons
- craft materials such as yarn, pom-poms, or cloth scraps
- glue

1. Glue two sheets of paper together on three edges. Leave one side open. Now do the same thing with two other sheets of paper.

2. Use crayons and craft materials to decorate your puppets.

3. Put a hand inside each opening. Work with a partner. Use your puppet to put on a puppet show about working together.

 # Fingerplay

Share the following fingerplay with children. Ask them to listen and watch as you read the words and perform the movements.

Working Together

There are lots of jobs **(pretend to do a household task such as sweeping)**

For a family to do. **(open rounded arms as if gathering family)**

When everyone works together **(point several times as if pointing to people in a circle)**

The work will soon be through. **(brush open palms together several times)**

After all the jobs are done, **(cross arms over chest)**

Everyone can have some fun! **(raise arms above head as if cheering)**

Provide children with a copy of the fingerplay on the following page. This simplified version of the fingerplay omits the movements, allowing children to focus on the text for the words they will say.

- Ask children to listen again and to track the print as you say the fingerplay.
- Repeat the fingerplay line by line, having children echo after you and perform the movements.
- After several readings, organize children into small groups. Tell the groups to select their own movements for the first line to show a job they do at home with their families.
- Invite groups to perform the fingerplay for classmates.

You may want to innovate on the fingerplay to make it about classroom jobs. In the second line, replace the words *a family* with *classmates*.

Name _____ Date _____

Fingerplay

Working Together

There are lots of jobs

For a family to do.

When everyone works together,

The work will soon be through.

After all the jobs are done,

Everyone can have some fun!

 # Song

Provide children with a copy of the song on the following page. Ask children to listen to you sing the song. Sing the words to the tune of "The Wheels on the Bus."

Ask children to listen again and to track the print as you sing. Repeat the song line by line, having children echo after you. Then ask children to join you in singing the entire verse.

Now ask children to brainstorm community helpers. Use the community helpers in additional verses for the song, such as:

> Police officers help us follow the law. Follow the law. Follow the law. Police officers help us follow the law. They work so hard for you.
>
> Firefighters help keep people safe.
>
> Garbage collectors pick up trash.
>
> Librarians check out books.
>
> Doctors help keep you well.
>
> Teachers help children learn.

- Organize children into small groups.
- Assign each group a specific community helper and have the group practice their verse.
- Bring the whole group together and sing the first verse.
- Have groups sing each verse about a specific helper. Then repeat the first verse.

Name _____ Date _____

 **Song**

Community Helpers Work for You
(Sung to the tune of "The Wheels on the Bus")

Community helpers

Work for you,

Work for you. Yes they do!

Community helpers

Work for you.

They have big jobs to do.

Unit Planner

Long-Term Project Pages 14–15	Materials Needed
Earth Book Children work in small groups to create an Earth shape book. **Time Needed:** 4 weeks **Strand:** Geography **Lesson Link:** Lessons 1, 2, 4, and 5	• colored construction paper and writing paper • scissors • crayons or markers
Geography Activity Pages 16–17	
The Bear Went over the Landforms Children play a game to help learn about landforms. **Time Needed:** 20–30 minutes **Strand:** Geography **Lesson Link:** Lessons 1 and 2	• scissors
Hands-On Activities Pages 18–19	
Activity 1 **Four-Seasons Circle** Children draw and tell about the four seasons of the year. **Time Needed:** 20–30 minutes **Strand:** Geography **Lesson Link:** Lesson 4	• white paper plates or big circles of construction paper • crayons • scissors • paste or glue
Activity 2 **Natural Resource Bracelet** Children make bracelets using natural resources. **Time Needed:** 20–30 minutes **Strand:** Geography **Lesson Link:** Lesson 3	• cotton yarn • strips of scrap paper • metal paper clips • paste or glue
Performance Activities Pages 20–23	
Activity 1 **Citizenship Cheer** Children write a cheer about the U.S.A. **Time Needed:** 20 minutes **Strand:** Citizenship **Lesson Link:** Lesson 6	none
Activity 2 **Prop Talk Plan** Children talk about objects made from natural resources. **Time Needed:** 20 minutes **Strand:** Economics **Lesson Link:** Lesson 3	• bags • items used from natural resources
For Personal Finance, see pp. 60–69; for Calendar Activities, see pp. 70–76.	

 Earth Book

Introduction

In this activity, children work in small groups to create an Earth shape book. The project takes four weeks to complete. You may follow the plan below to organize the project.

MATERIALS

- colored construction paper and writing paper
- scissors
- crayons or markers

Project Plan

Week 1: Begin a Book About Earth 30 minutes

Explain to children that they will be working together to make a shape book about Earth. You may wish to show children a model that has a cover decorated to resemble Earth, with blank pages of writing paper inside.

For each small group, cut out a colored-paper cover and at least six pages of writing paper. Keep the pages loose, giving groups just one at a time as needed.

To get children started on their shape books, preview the lessons with them. Write the following topics on the board. Have the group write the lesson headings on a book page to serve as the table of contents for their book.

Earth

- The Earth's Land
- The Earth's Water
- Cities and Towns
- Seasons
- Caring for the Earth's Land and Water

To prompt discussion, you may want to ask questions such as these:

- Does all the land on Earth look the same? How is it different?
- Look at a map of the world. Does there seem to be more land or water? How much more?
- Do you live in a city or a town? What is the difference?
- What are the different parts of the year? What is something that you like to do during each season?
- Why do people need to take care of land and water? What can you do to help?

For the rest of the week, allow groups to work on pages of their books.

Weeks 2 and 3: Add Information to the Book 30 minutes

Encourage children to add more details and information to their pages. Suggest that they use the vocabulary from the lessons in their pages. Remind children to include an illustration for each topic in their book. You may want to direct children to write a label or caption for each picture.

Week 4: Assemble the Book 30 minutes

Have groups work together to make the cover of their book. Remind them to include a title and the names of all the authors of the book. After all the pages are complete, help children bind their pages together. You may want to staple the pages together, or you may punch holes in the pages and tie them with yarn.

Put the completed books on display. Encourage children to read the books during independent reading time.

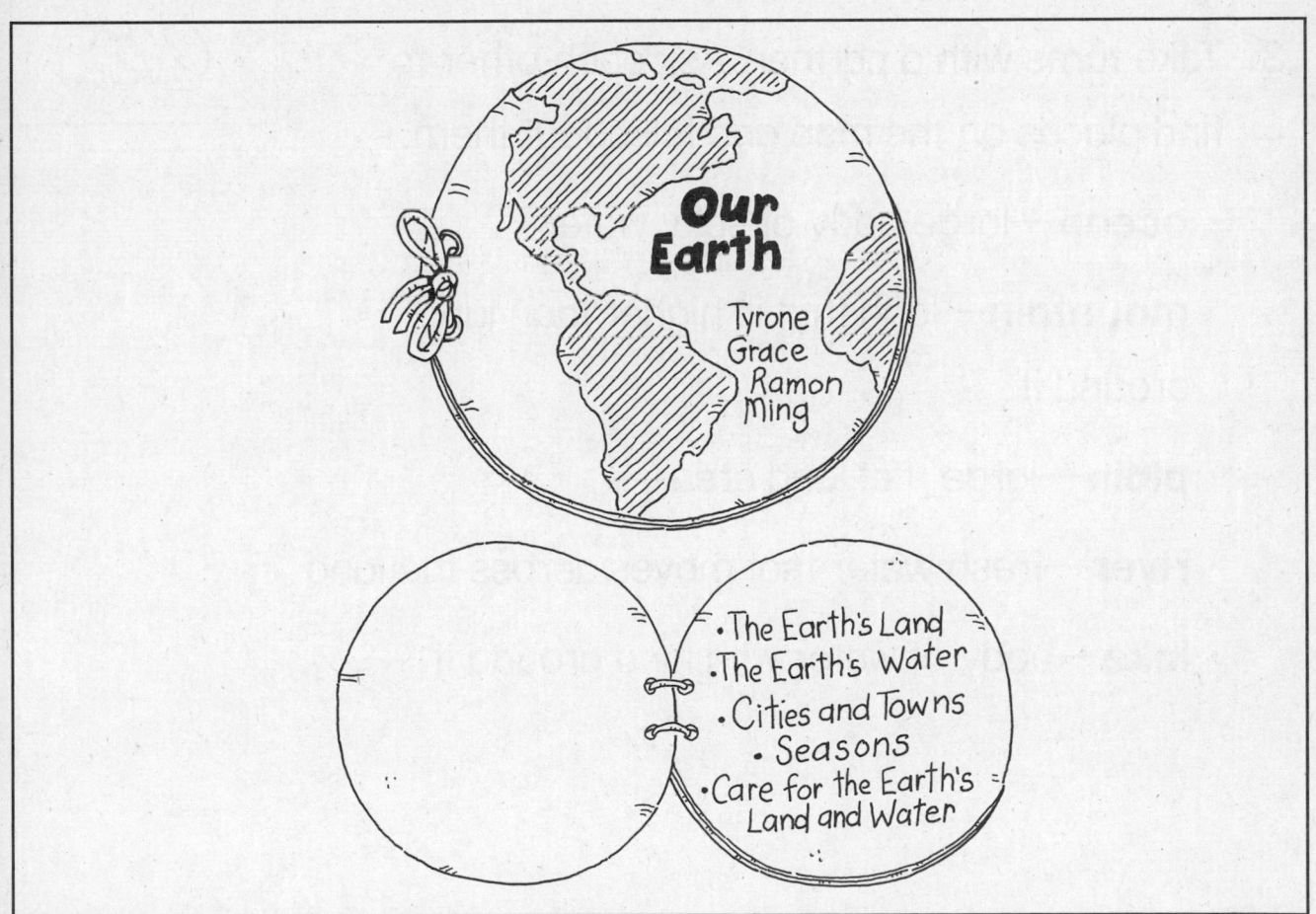

Name _____   Date _____

The Bear Went over the Landforms

Sing "The Bear Went over the Mountain."
Now play a game in which the bear goes
over **plains, rivers, lakes,** and **oceans**
too!

MATERIALS
• scissors

1. Cut out the bear.

2. Read about the landforms.

3. Take turns with a partner. Ask each other to
   find places on the map and tell about them.

   • **ocean**—large body of salty water

   • **mountain**—land that is higher than land
     around it

   • **plain**—large, flat land area

   • **river**—fresh water that moves across the land

   • **lake**—body of water with land around it

16   Use with *School and Family*, **Unit 2**

Name _____ Date _____

The Bear Went over the Landforms

Here's an example of how to play.

Player 1 says, "The bear went over the ocean."

Player 2 moves the bear to the ocean. Then Player 2 says, "The ocean is a large body of salty water."

Name _____ Date _____

Four-Seasons Circle

Think about things you do in each
season. Draw pictures of your ideas.

MATERIALS
- white paper plates or big circles of construction paper
- crayons
- scissors
- paste or glue

1. On your pie plate, draw four lines to make four equal parts.

2. Draw a picture in each part to show what you do in each season. Put the seasons in order.

3. Paste the season names on the plate.

4. Tell a partner what you do in each season.

spring
summer
fall
winter

winter   spring

fall   summer

Name _____ Date _____

Natural Resource Bracelet

Make a bracelet from materials made from natural resources. Use yarn made from a cotton plant. Use paper made from trees. Use metal paper clips. Metal comes from mines.

When you look at your bracelet, remember to use natural resources wisely!

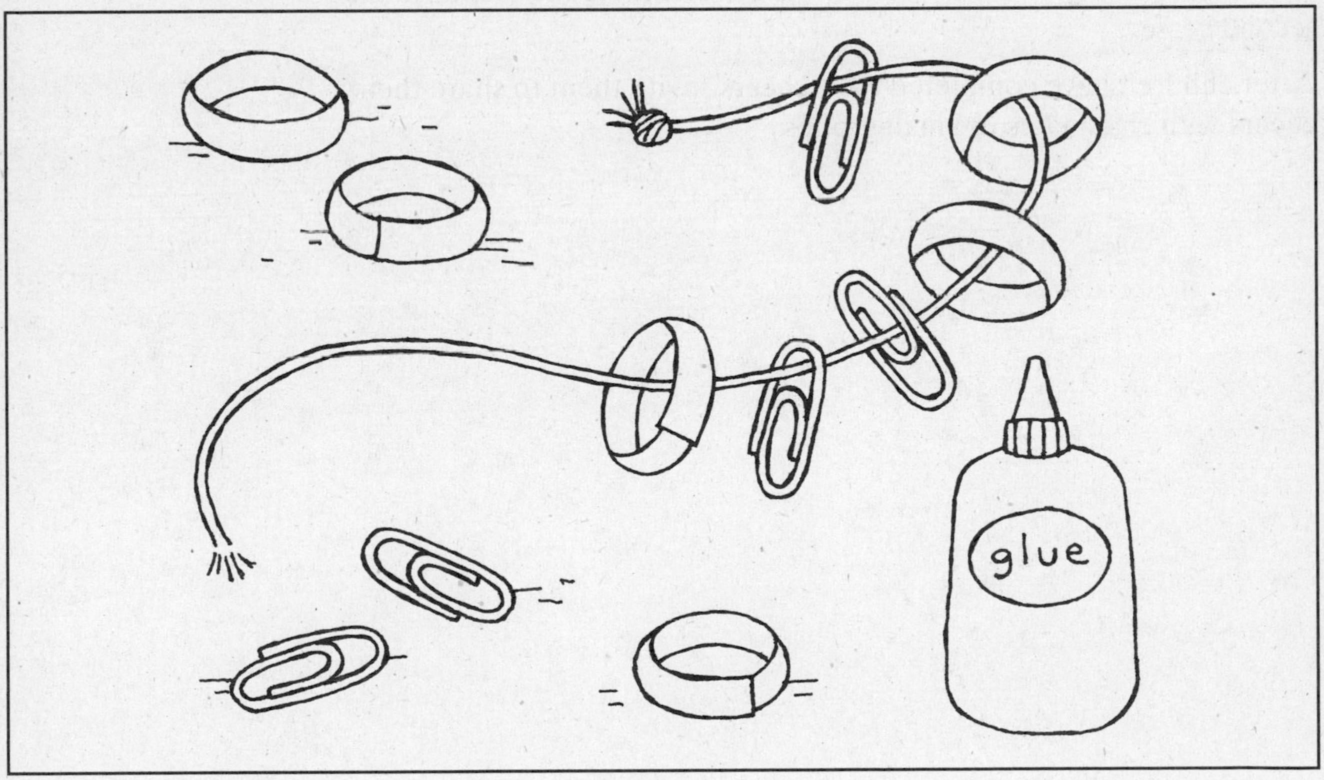

MATERIALS

- cotton yarn
- strips of scrap paper
- metal paper clips
- paste or glue

glue

Citizenship Cheer

Invite children to complete the cheer about their country and state on the following page. Remind children that the name of their country is the United States of America, which is sometimes called by its initials, the U.S. or U.S.A. Invite children to discuss things that make our country special, such as the flag and the Statue of Liberty. Have them list other things they know about our country.

Write the name of your state on the board to assist children with spelling. To help children get started, guide them in brainstorming a list of things that your state is associated with, such as:

- special places
- industries
- natural resources
- cultural activities

Children will use the words from this list to complete the blanks in the second verse.

After children have completed their cheers, invite them to share their cheers with classmates or small groups.

Name _____ Date _____

Citizenship Cheer

Let's hear it for the U.S.A. _____

Hooray for the _____!

Hooray for the _____!

Hooray for the _____!

    Let's hear it for _____, our great state!

    Hooray for _____!

    Hooray for _____!

    Hooray for _____!

 # Prop Talk Plan

Invite children to give a prop talk on natural resources. To help children prepare for their prop talks, review Core Lesson 3 and Extend Lesson 3 about natural resources. Then have them complete the Prop Plan on page 23. Discuss items that they could write on each bag. Then they can use these bags to help them with their prop talk.

MATERIALS

- bags
- items used from natural resources

Prepare several gift bags with items that represent different gifts from Earth. Children will use these items to enhance their talk.

Gifts from Trees: small wooden toys, a note pad, pencil, book

Gifts from Plants: peanuts in the shell; cotton clothing items; jars of berry jam

Gifts from Underground: things made of metal, such as paper clips, scissors, kitchen silverware, or small tools

Gifts from Rivers and Lakes: bottle of drinking water, or salmon

You may wish to model giving a prop talk.

> *A natural resource is something in nature that people use to live. Natural resources are like gifts from Earth. There are different kinds of natural resources.*

Choose an object from one bag. Talk about what it is, where it comes from, and how people use it.

Invite children to give a talk about gifts from Earth choosing one of the props from the bag. Tell them to begin their talks by explaining what natural resources are. They should then choose one item from one bag and tell what it is, what resource it comes from, and how people use it.

Name _____   Date _____

 **Prop Talk Plan**

What are natural resources?

_____

_____

How do people use each kind of gift from Earth? Write your answers on each bag.

23   Use with *School and Family,* Unit 2

Unit Planner

Long-Term Project Pages 26–27	Materials Needed

Create a Class Store
 	
Children create a class store and role-play buyers and sellers.
 	
Time Needed: 4 weeks   **Strand:** Economics
 	
Lesson Link: Lessons 2, 3, and 4
	• variety of craft materials, such as clay, paper, and cardboard
	• markers
	    • blank index cards
	    • yarn
	    • play money

Geography Activities Pages 28–29	
Activity 1 **Goods and Services Map** Children make a map of places that sell goods and give services. **Time Needed:** 20–30 minutes **Strand:** Geography **Lesson Link:** Lesson 2	none
Activity 2 **Plan Places for New Services** Children plan where new community services should be built. **Time Needed:** 20–30 minutes **Strand:** Geography **Lesson Link:** Lesson 1	• scissors • glue
Hands-On Activities Pages 30–31	

Activity 1 **Better Butter Factory**
 	
Children make butter from scratch.
 	
Time Needed: 20–30 minutes   **Strand:** Economics
 	
Lesson Link: Lessons 4 and 5
	• small glass jar with lid
	• whipping cream
	    • strainer
	    • saltine crackers
	    • butter spreader

Activity 2 **Butter Booklet** Children put together a booklet about how butter is made. **Time Needed:** 20–30 minutes **Strand:** Economics **Lesson Link:** Lessons 4 and 5	• crayons and markers • scissors • glue
Performance Activities Pages 32–35	
Activity 1 **Chalk Talk** Children give chalk talks to summarize lessons in the unit. **Time Needed:** 20 minutes **Strand:** Economics **Lesson Link:** Lessons 1, 2, 3, 4, and 5	none
Activity 2 **Choral Reading** Children give a choral reading of a poem about workers. **Time Needed:** 20 minutes **Strand:** Economics **Lesson Link:** Lesson 4	none
For Personal Finance, see pp. 60–69; for Calendar Activities, see pp. 70–76.	

Create a Class Store

Introduction

In this activity, children work together to create a class store. They then use the class store to role-play store workers and shoppers.

MATERIALS

- variety of craft materials, such as clay, paper, and cardboard
- markers
- blank index cards
- yarn
- play money

Project Plan

Week 1: Plan the Store 30 minutes

Explain to children that they will be working together to create a class store. They will make items to buy and sell in the store. They will use play money that you provide. They will take turns being buyers and sellers.

Draw on children's experiences to guide them in making an overall plan for the store. Prompt the discussion with questions such as the following:

- When you go to a store, what kind of workers do you see?
- What other kinds of workers are needed to make a store run smoothly?
- What does it mean to be a good shopper?
- What do you do in a store after you find the things you want to buy?

Have children select a name for their class store. You may wish to take several suggestions and have children vote for one.

Week 2: Make Items for Store 60 minutes

Explain to children that they will work in small groups to make items to sell in the class store. Share with them the variety of craft materials available to them. Each group will select an item to make and then will make multiples of it to put in the store. You may want to brainstorm things for children to make, such as bookmarks, craft-stick treasure boxes, refrigerator magnets, and picture frames. Allow children time to create their items. Help them price the items appropriately.

Week 3: Discuss Jobs for Store 30 minutes

Lead children in a discussion about the various jobs that will need to be performed to set up the store and sell the items. Make a list of jobs, such as shelf stocker, display clerk, sales clerk, check-out clerk, and store manager. Use blank index cards and yarn to create necklaces identifying each job. Discuss the roles of each worker. Then have children take turns role-playing various workers and shoppers.

Week 4: Role-Play Workers and Shoppers 60 minutes

Distribute the play money and review the amounts of currency with children. Review the responsibilities of the jobs shown on the job necklaces. Then have small groups of children take turns being workers and shoppers in the school store, with workers wearing the necklaces. If you have store inventory available after each child has had an opportunity to be a shopper, you may wish to invite other classes to visit the store. Provide play money they can use to shop.

 **Goods and Services Map**

Look at each place on the community map.

Label places that sell goods with **G**.

Label places that give services with **S**.

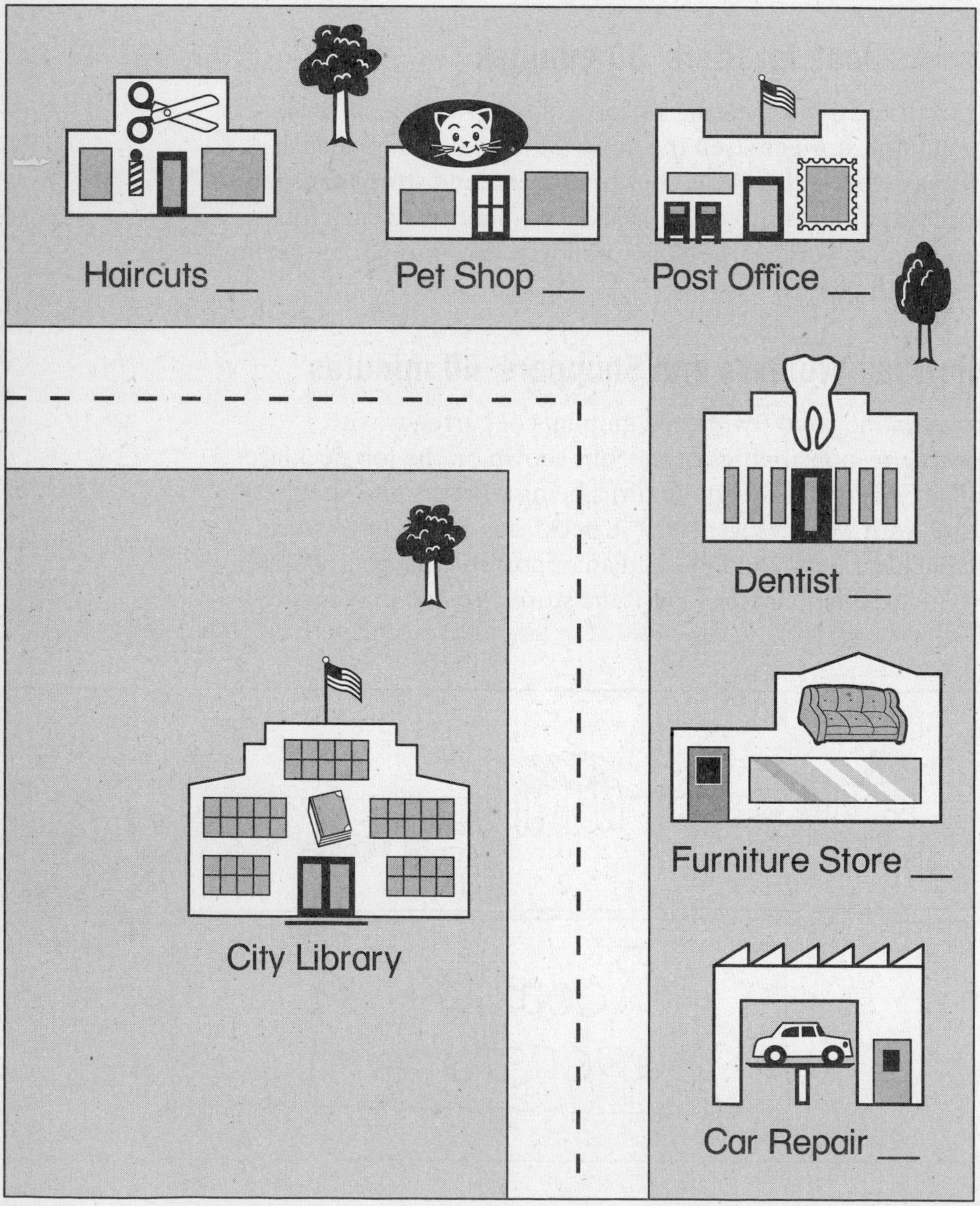

Haircuts __

Pet Shop __

Post Office __

Dentist __

City Library

Furniture Store __

Car Repair __

Name _____ Date _____

Plan Places for New Services

This community needs three new services. Choose a good place for each one. Glue its picture on the map. Tell why you put each service where you did.

MATERIALS
- scissors
- glue

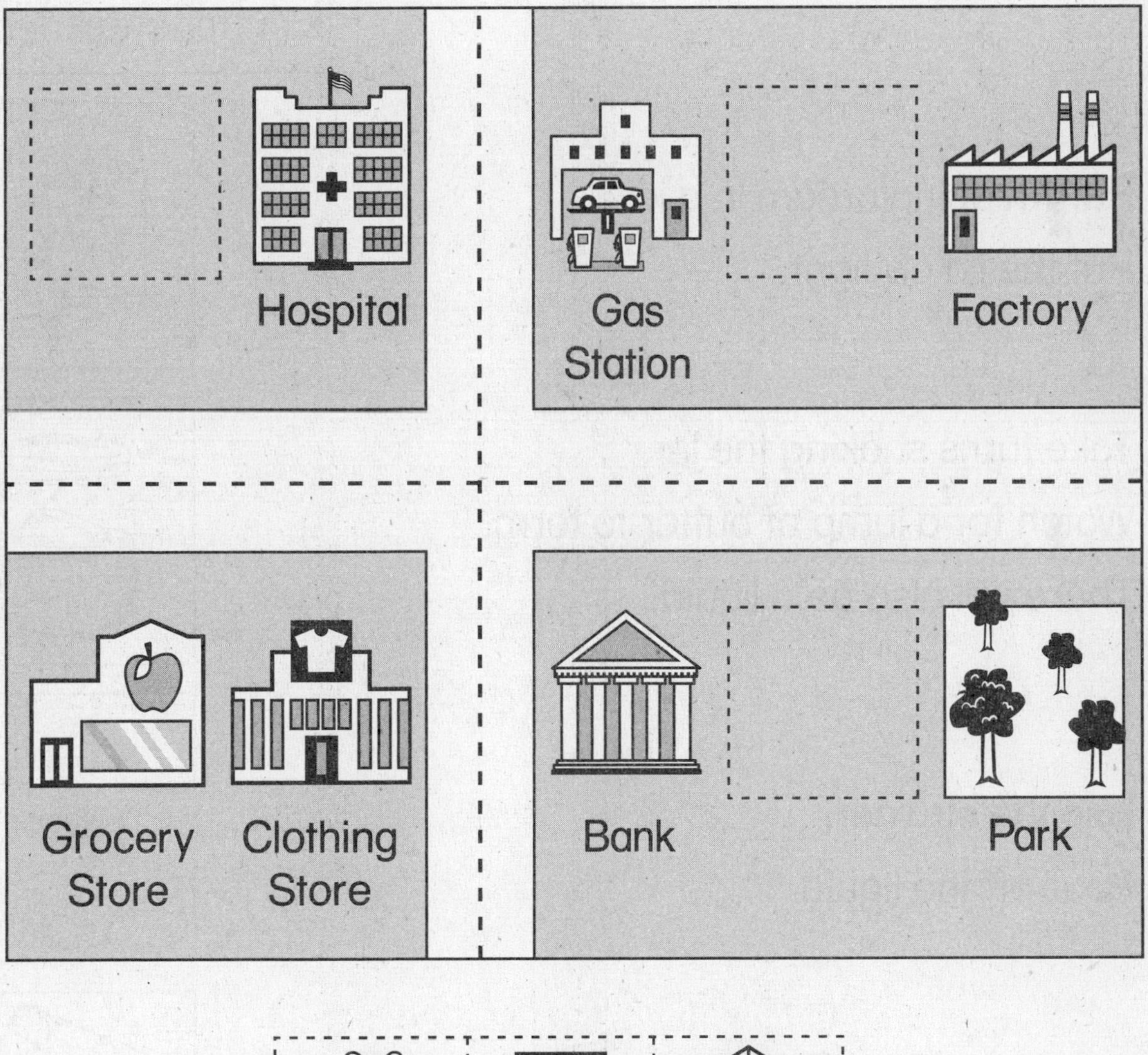

Hospital	Gas Station · Factory
Grocery Store · Clothing Store	Bank · Park

Daycare Center · Doctor's Office · Fire Station

Name _____ Date _____

 **Better Butter Factory**

Note to Teachers: *Be sure to check for food allergies before doing this activity.*

How is butter made? Let's find out!

Work with a small group.

MATERIALS
- small glass jar with lid
- whipping cream
- strainer
- saltine crackers
- butter spreader

1. Put whipping cream in a jar.
   Put the lid on tight.

2. Take turns shaking the jar.
   Watch for a lump of butter to form.
   There will also be a liquid.

3. Use the strainer.
   Pour off the liquid.

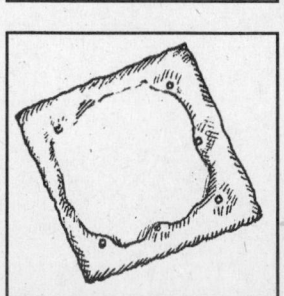

4. Spread the butter on a cracker. Enjoy!

Name _____ Date _____

 # Butter Booklet

Make a book about butter. Cut out the sentence strips. Paste each strip on a sheet of paper. Draw a picture to go with each sentence. Put the pages in order. Make a cover.

MATERIALS
- crayons and markers
- scissors
- glue

1. First, dairy farmers raise cows to give milk.

2. Next, trucks take the milk from the farm to a factory.

3. At the factory, part of the milk is used to make butter.

4. Then other trucks take the butter to stores.

5. After that, people buy butter at the store.

6. Finally, people eat the butter!

Bringing Social Studies Alive

31

Use with *School and Family,* Unit 3

 # Chalk Talk

Invite children to give a chalk talk to summarize one of the lessons in the unit. In a chalk talk, children use words and drawings to share what they learned about a topic. As they talk, children will draw on the chalkboard. Alternatively, you could have children draw on white boards or chart tablets.

Before children present their chalk talks, help them make a plan using the steps below and the planner on the following page.

- Have children select a topic. Review the choices from the unit, such as wants and needs, goods and services, or how foods get to market.

- Have children complete the planner. Encourage them to make practice sketches on the back of the page.

- Organize children into small groups. Have each member present a chalk talk. After each presentation, encourage group members to comment on something that the speaker did exceptionally well during the chalk talk.

Name _____ Date _____

 ## Chalk Talk Planner

I will talk about _____.

> **I will begin with a question. I will ask the listeners this question:**
>
> _____.

Here are two things I will tell about in my talk.

1. _____

_____

2. _____

_____

> **I will draw pictures to show what I am talking about. (Use the back of this page to draw.)**

> **I will let the listeners know my talk is over. I will say**
>
> _____
>
> _____.

Choral Reading

Share the following poem with children. Model reading with emphasis and enthusiasm.

Work, Work, Work!

Work, work, work!

People work in factories

And in offices too.

There are all kinds of jobs

For many people to do!

People work in stores

And on the streets too.

There are all kinds of jobs

For many people to do!

People work at schools

And at homes too.

There are all kinds of jobs

For many people to do!

Work, work, work!

Provide children with a copy of the poem on the following page. Work with children to read the poem fluently. With less fluent readers, have them echo each line after you. Remind all children that they can use their voice to make the reading more interesting for the listener. Reread the poem, asking children to listen for pauses and words you emphasize. Explain that fluent readers make their reading sound as if they were simply talking to someone else.

After several readings, organize children into small groups, pairing less fluent readers with more fluent ones. Have groups practice reading the poem together. Invite groups to perform a choral reading for the class.

 **Choral Reading**

Work, Work, Work!

Work, work, work!

People work in factories

And in offices too.

There are all kinds of jobs

For many people to do!

People work in stores

And on the streets too.

There are all kinds of jobs

For many people to do!

People work at schools

And at homes too.

There are all kinds of jobs

For many people to do!

Work, work, work!

Bringing Social Studies Alive
35
Use with *School and Family*, Unit 3

Unit Planner

Long-Term Project Pages 38–39	Materials Needed
Create an Exhibit Children research how people lived long ago in order to create a classroom exhibit. **Time Needed:** 4 weeks **Strand:** History **Lesson Link:** Lessons 1 and 3	• craft materials, such as clay, boxes, craft sticks, and fabric scraps • drawing paper • crayons or markers • age-appropriate nonfiction books about the past
Geography Activities Pages 40–41	
Activity 1 **Make a Map** Children make a map like the ones the early American settlers used. **Time Needed:** 20–30 minutes **Strand:** Geography **Lesson Link:** Lesson 3	• scissors • glue • brown paper bag or brown paper
Activity 2 **Transportation Graph** The class makes a graph of the kinds of transportation the children use. **Time Needed:** 20–30 minutes **Strand:** Geography **Lesson Link:** Lesson 5	• scissors • glue
Hands-On Activities Pages 42–43	
Activity 1 **Personal History Timeline** Children make a timeline of their life. **Time Needed:** 20–30 minutes **Strand:** History **Lesson Link:** Lesson 1	• crayons, markers
Activity 2 **Make a Toss-and-Catch Game** Children play a game that American Indians enjoyed. **Time Needed:** 20–30 minutes **Strand:** History **Lesson Link:** Lesson 2	• string, 18" long • large rubber band • unsharpened pencil
Performance Activities Pages 44–47	
Activity 1 **Pilgrim Talk** Children learn the words and phrases that the Pilgrims used. **Time Needed:** 20 minutes **Strand:** History **Lesson Link:** Lesson 3	none
Activity 2 **The Lost Mouser** Children put on a play about a Pilgrim girl's missing cat. **Time Needed:** 20 minutes **Strand:** History **Lesson Link:** Lesson 4	none
For Personal Finance, see pp. 60–69; for Calendar Activities, see pp. 70–76.	

Bringing Social Studies Alive
37
Use with *School and Family*, Unit 4

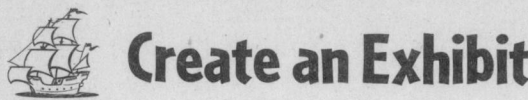

Create an Exhibit

Introduction

In this activity, children work together to create an exhibit about life long ago.

The project takes four weeks to complete. You may follow the plan below to organize the project.

MATERIALS

- craft materials, such as clay, boxes, craft sticks, and fabric scraps
- drawing paper
- crayons or markers
- age-appropriate nonfiction books about the past

Project Plan
Week 1: Research Facts About the Past 30 minutes

Tell children that they will be working together to create a class museum exhibit about life long ago in the United States. You may want to introduce the term *historian*, explaining that a historian is someone who studies history, or stories about the past. Point out that children will be historians as they work on the museum exhibit, doing research about the past and creating displays for the museum. Explain to children that their exhibit will be arranged in different sections: transportation long ago, clothing long ago, and houses long ago.

Point out to children that they will have to do research to find out facts about the past. They can use the information they find to create pictures and models for their exhibit. Explain that museums usually display some information along with the things on display. Tell children that they can write labels and captions to go with each of the items on display.

Work with small groups to show them how to use age-appropriate resources to find out facts about transportation long ago. Provide an assortment of nonfiction books and children's encyclopedias, as available. Model how to write captions for pictures.

Have small groups begin their research on transportation and work on items, either pictures or models, for display in the exhibit.

Suggest that children conduct research interviews at home. Tell them to ask adults in their families to teach them songs or games that the adults played as children. Explain that children will have an opportunity to share these songs and games with the class during the exhibit. You might also want to send a note home to ask families to loan real objects, such as clothing from long ago, to add to the displays.

Week 2: Research Clothing Styles 30 minutes

Have children use the nonfiction reference materials to research clothing long ago, giving assistance as needed. Encourage them to use what they learned to draw a picture or craft a model to represent clothing styles of the past. Remind them to sum up facts they learned and write a few sentences to serve as a caption for their display.

Week 3: Research Homes of Long Ago 30 minutes

Have children use the nonfiction reference materials to research homes of long ago, giving assistance as needed. Encourage them to use what they learned to draw a picture or craft a model to represent homes of the past. Remind them to sum up facts they learned and write a few sentences to serve as a caption for their display.

Week 4: Create the Exhibits 30 minutes

Guide children in setting up their exhibit. Invite small groups to tour the exhibit. Remind children that museum visitors are not allowed to touch most displays in real museums, and ask them to follow that rule for the classroom exhibit. Remind them to pause to read the facts with the displays. As part of the exhibit, invite children who learned songs or games from family members to share them with the class. You may want to invite visitors, such as family members, school workers, or other classes to view the display.

 **Make a Map**

Make a map like the ones the early settlers of America used.

1. Draw a dotted line to show how to travel from England to North America.

2. Cut out the ship and glue it near the line.

3. Cut a paper bag apart to make it flat. Crumple it to make it look old. Then paste your map to it.

4. Then tell what your map shows.

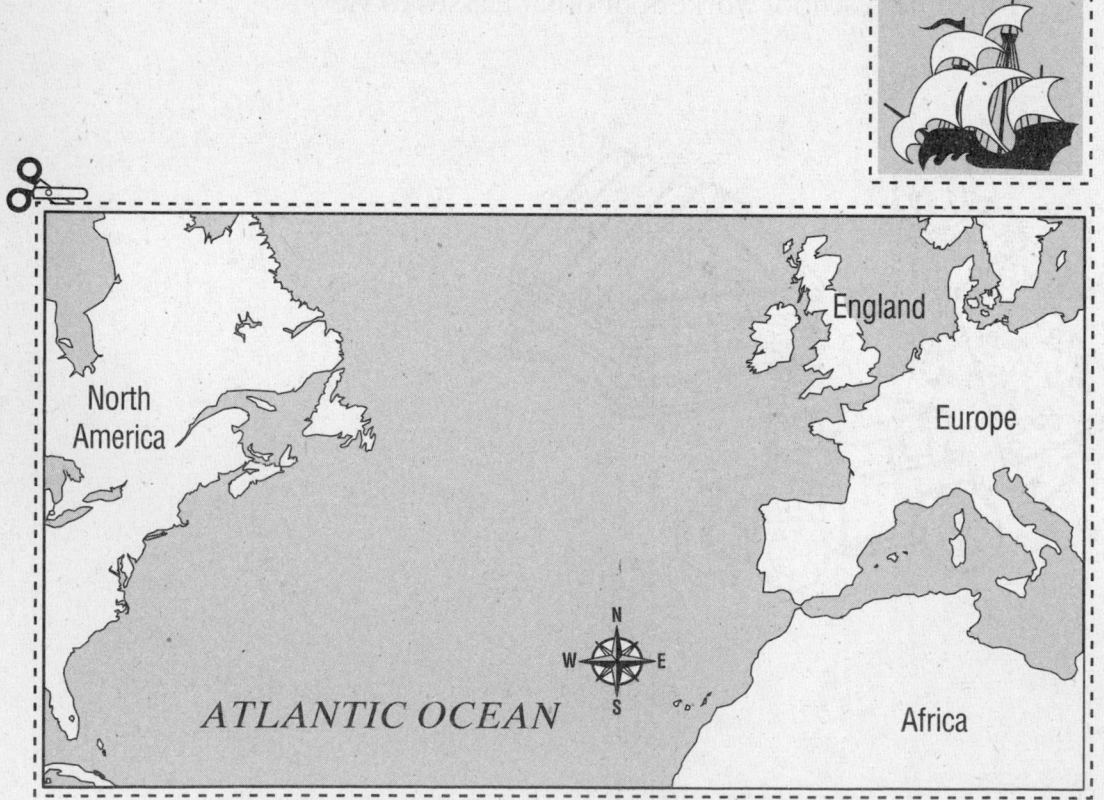

Transportation Graph

How do you get from place to place? Look at the pictures below. Cut out the pictures of transportation you have used. Glue your pictures on a class graph.

Which form of transportation does the class use the most? The least? Would a graph of long ago be different from your graph?

MATERIALS
• scissors
• glue

How We Get from Place to Place

horse	bus	car	truck	train	subway	ferry	airplane

Name _____ Date _____

HANDS ON ACTIVITY

Personal History Timeline

• crayons, markers

You have a history of
your own! Think about:

- people in your family

- places you lived

- things you learned to do

- places you visited

- your friends

- your pets

Make a timeline of your life.

Draw pictures about yourself.

Personal History Timeline

Born
Age 1
Age 2
Age 3
Age 4
Age 5
Age 6
Age 7

Name _____ Date _____

Make a Toss-and-Catch Game

Many groups of American Indians played toss-and-catch games. You can make a toss-and-catch game to play!

1. Tie the string about 2 inches from one end of the pencil.

2. Tie the rubber band to the other end of the string.

3. Swing the rubber band out and up. Try to catch it on the pencil. Once you get very good at catching with one hand, switch to the other hand.

MATERIALS

- string, 18" long
- large rubber band
- unsharpened pencil

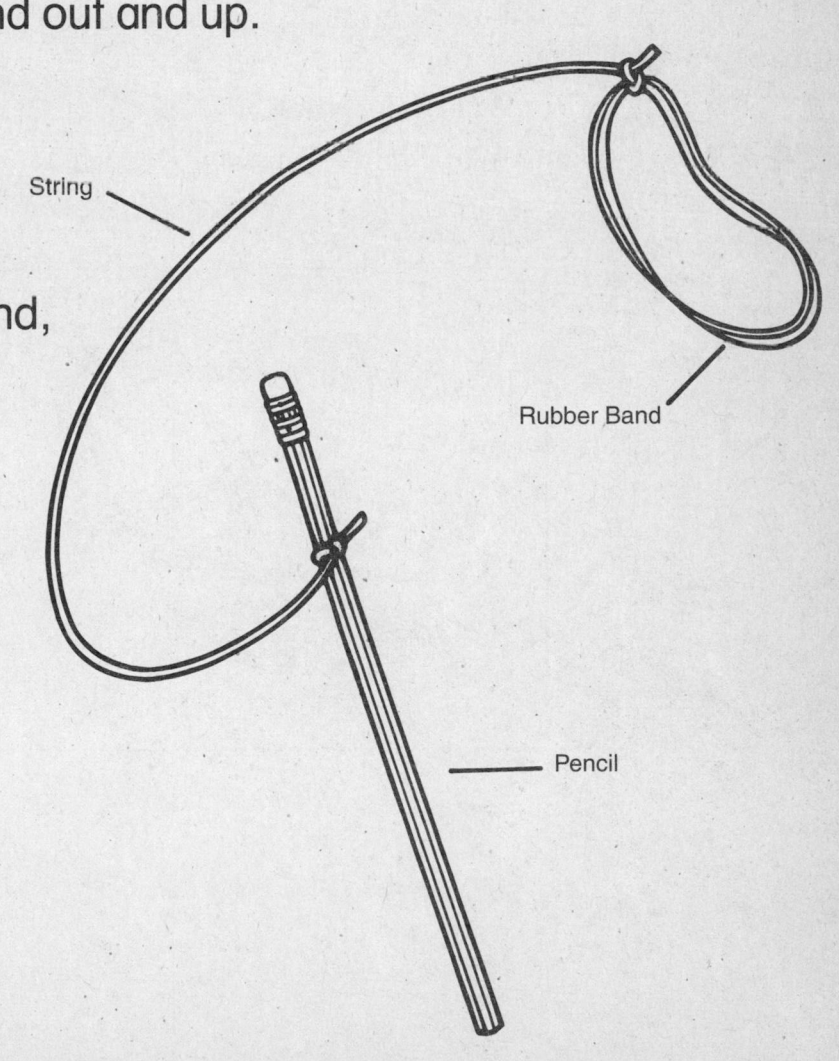

String

Rubber Band

Pencil

Bringing Social Studies Alive

43

Use with *School and Family*, Unit 4

Pilgrim Talk

Distribute the chart on page 45 to children. First, read the chart to children and then have them echo each phrase the Pilgrims used. Next, say:

- We say "How are you?" What did Pilgrims say? (What cheer?) Saying "What cheer?" is like saying "What's the good news?"

- We say "Goodbye!" What did Pilgrims say? (Fare thee well) This was a way of saying "Good Luck!"

- We say "cat." What did Pilgrims say? (mouser) Pilgrims could not go to a supermarket. They grew their food in the summer and kept it in a special place all through the winter. The mouser's job was to catch any mouse that tried to eat the stored food.

- We say "stew." What did Pilgrims say? (pottage) It got its name because it was cooked in a pot.

- We say "fireplace." What did Pilgrims say? (hearth) Some children may not be familiar with wood-burning fireplaces. Explain that Pilgrims cooked food over the fire in the hearth. The wood burned and became gray ashes.

- We say "skirt." What did Pilgrims say? (petticoat)

- We say "pants." What did Pilgrims say? (breeches)

Name _____ Date _____

 # Pilgrim Talk

We say:	Pilgrims said:
How are you?	What cheer?
Goodbye!	Fare thee well!
cat	mouser
stew	pottage
pants	breeches
fireplace	hearth
skirt	petticoat

 # The Lost Mouser

Pilgrims called their cats "mousers." The cat's job was to keep every mouse away from the Pilgrim house.

Cast of Characters

John: a Pilgrim boy

Ann: John's friend

Tom: John's brother

Mother: the mother of John and Tom

A Mouser

Setting

The home of John and his family.

[Ann knocks at John's door.]

John: What cheer, Ann?

Ann: Oh, John! I have lost my mouser.

John: What color is your mouser?

Ann: My mouser is white.

Mother *[calls to John and Tom]:* A mouser is in here! Get out, mouser!

Name _____ Date _____

Tom: Get out, mouser!

Mouser: Meow.

[Ann comes into the house.]

Ann: Where is the mouser?

Mother: It is in the hearth! It wants our pottage!

Mouser: Meow.

Ann: Is it white? My mouser is white.

Tom: No, this mouser is gray.

John: The fire is out. The hearth is not hot. We can get the mouser out.

[Ann and John pull the cat out of the hearth.]

Mouser: Meow! Meow!

Ann: Oh, no! There are gray ashes on the mouser! Now my petticoat is gray!

John: My breeches are gray!

Tom: Now the mouser is white!

Mouser: Meow.

Ann *[pets the cat's head]:* This *is* my mouser! I will take my mouser home. Fare thee well.

Unit Planner

Long-Term Project Pages 50–51	Materials Needed
City and State Class Book Children create a class book about their city and state. **Time Needed:** 4 weeks **Strand:** Citizenship **Lesson Link:** Lessons 2 and 5	• craft materials, such as clay, boxes, craft sticks, and fabric scraps • drawing paper • crayons or markers • age-appropriate reference materials
Geography Activity Pages 52–53	
Laws and Signs Children glue signs where they belong on the map. **Time Needed:** 20–30 minutes **Strand:** Geography **Lesson Link:** Lesson 1	• scissors • glue
Hands-On Activities Pages 54–55	
Activity 1 **Make an Award Ribbon** Children make ribbons honoring heroes in the community. **Time Needed:** 20–30 minutes **Strand:** Citizenship **Lesson Link:** Lesson 4	• crayons, colored pencils, markers
Activity 2 **U.S.A. Symbol Pop-up** Children make pop up cards with symbols of the United States. **Time Needed:** 20–30 minutes **Strand:** Citizenship **Lesson Link:** Lesson 5	• construction paper • glue • scissors • crayons
Performance Activities Pages 56–59	
Activity 1 **Meet a Hero or Leader** Children give talks about important people from the lesson. **Time Needed:** 20 minutes **Strand:** Citizenship **Lesson Link:** Lessons 2 and 4	none
Activity 2 **Lion for Mayor! Mouse for Mayor!** Children put on a play about a lion and mouse who are running for mayor. **Time Needed:** 20 minutes **Strand:** Citizenship **Lesson Link:** Lesson 3	none
For Personal Finance, see pp. 60–69; for Calendar Activities, see pp. 70–76.	

City and State Class Book

Introduction

In this activity, children work together to create a class book about their city and state.

The project takes four weeks to complete. You may follow the plan below to organize the project.

Project Plan
Week 1: Research Local Information 30 minutes

Tell children that they will be working together to create a class book that features information about their city or town and state. Explain to children that sometimes fact books share information in a question-and-answer format. If possible, share an example of an age-appropriate question-and-answer book. Tell children that you will pose the questions for the book and it will be up to them to find out the answers.

Lead children in a discussion about ways to find out information about their city or town and state. Have them brainstorm sources of information available to them. Record children's suggestions on chart paper and display it in the room for children to refer to as they conduct their research. Point out the importance of being able to verify facts as accurate before writing them in the book.

Organize children into small groups to begin their research. Write the following questions on chart paper and display them throughout the week.

books

newspapers

magazine articles

Internet

phone calls to interview people

- **Who is the leader of our town?**
- **What are some special places to visit in our town?**

Provide resources for children to use in their research. As groups work together, circulate to guide their discussions and work. Have children write the answers to the questions.

At the end of the week, bring children together to discuss their answers to the questions. Record the question on one page of the book. Record the class answer on a second page. Assign a group to illustrate the pages for the book.

Designate a place to put completed book pages throughout the following weeks.

Week 2: Research State Information 30 minutes

Write the following questions on chart paper and display them throughout the week.

- **Who is the governor of <name of your state>?**
- **What are some special places to visit in <name of your state>?**

Help children conduct research to find out the answers to these questions.

Week 3: Research State Symbols 30 minutes

Write the following questions on index cards and assign a question to each small group:

- **How does <name of your state> look on a map?**
- **What is the state flower of <name of your state>?**
- **What is the state tree of <name of your state>?**
- **What is the name of the state bird of <name of your state>?**
- **How does the flag of <name of your state> look?**

Have groups complete research to answer their question. Give assistance as needed. Direct children to work together to write and illustrate two pages for the class book, one that poses the question and one that provides the answer.

Week 4: Assemble the Book 30 minutes

Guide children in assembling their city and state book. You may want to divide a piece of poster paper into five sections, such as a circle in the middle and a square in each corner, and have groups decorate a section of the cover for the book. Read the book aloud to the class. Place the book in the classroom library so children can read the book independently.

 # Laws and Signs

Look at the signs! Sometimes signs tell about laws. Read where the signs go. Then glue the signs onto the map on page 53.

MATERIALS
- scissors
- glue

1. Put a STOP sign on each corner.

2. Put a DO NOT ENTER sign near the school driveway on Plum Street.

3. Put a NO PARKING sign across the street from the school on Plum Street.

4. Put a SCHOOL ZONE sign on Third Avenue before the crosswalk.

Name ____________________ Date ____________

GEOGRAPHY ACTIVITY

Laws and Signs

Read the directions on page 52.

Glue the signs on the map.

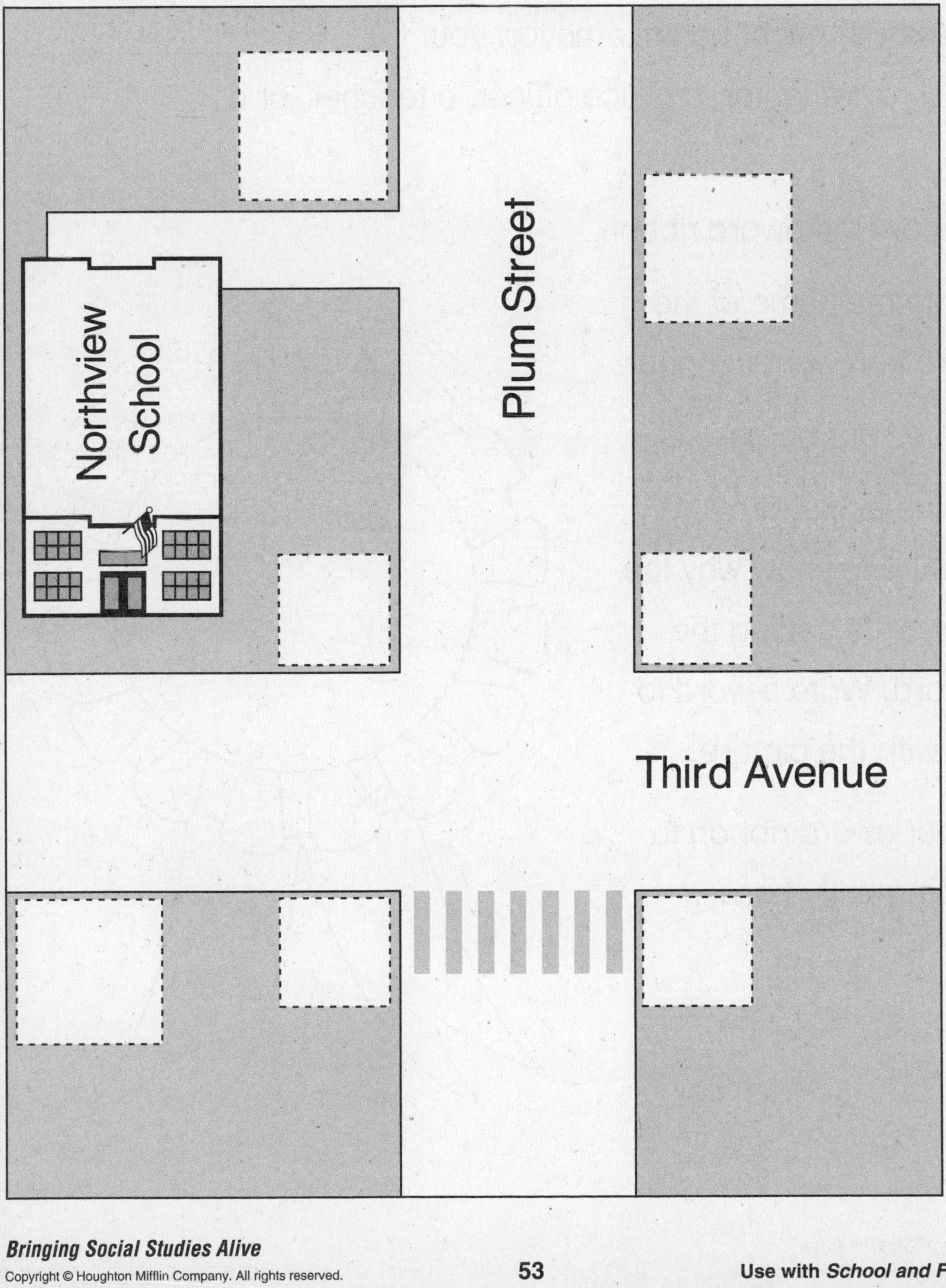
Northview School
Plum Street
Third Avenue

Name _____ Date _____

Make an Award Ribbon

Hip, hip, hooray for the heroes in your community! Choose a hero in your community. It might be your mayor, your principal, a firefighter, a police officer, a teacher, or a parent.

MATERIALS

- crayons, colored pencils, markers

1. Cut out the award ribbon.

2. Write the name of the hero you want to honor.

3. Write your name.

4. In the circle, draw a picture to show why the person is getting the award. Write a word to go with the picture.

Give your award ribbon to your community hero.

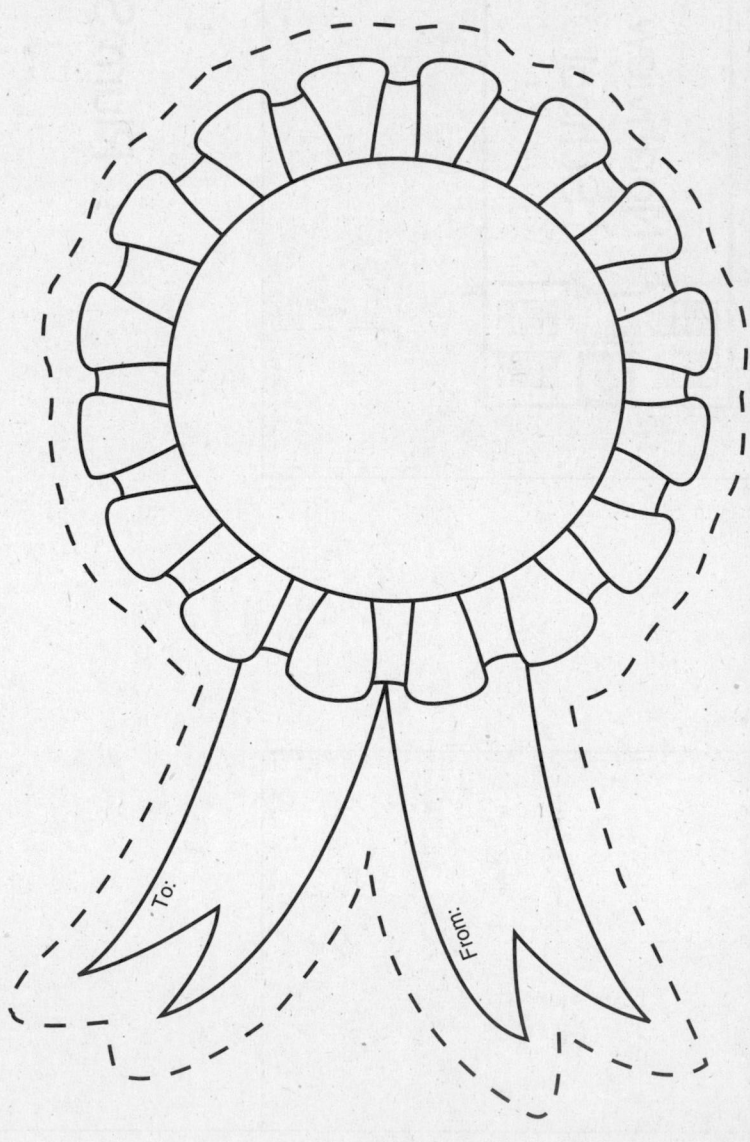

Bringing Social Studies Alive

Use with *School and Family*, Unit 5

🇺🇸 U.S.A. Symbol Pop-up

What do you picture when someone says "U.S.A."? There are many things that stand for our country. Make a pop-up card with a symbol of the United States.

MATERIALS
- construction paper
- scissors
- glue
- crayons

1. Fold your paper in half, top to bottom.

2. Cut two slits on the fold in the middle of the page. Make the slits one inch long. Make the slits one inch apart. You now have a tab.

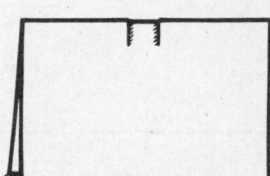

3. Look at the picture. Push the tab through to the inside of the card.

4. On another piece of paper, draw, color, and cut out a symbol of the U.S.A. It should fit inside the card.

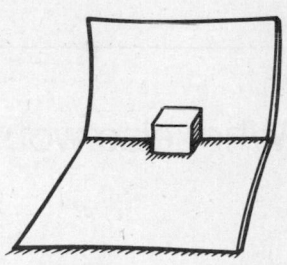

5. Open your card. Glue your symbol to the side of the tab.

6. Decorate your card with words and pictures.

I love the U.S.A.!

Name _____ Date _____

 # Meet a Leader or Hero

Choose a person from Lesson 2 or Lesson 4. Give a brief talk about the person. Use this form to plan your talk.

What is the person's name?

_____

Why is the person important?

_____

What do you find most interesting about this person?

_____

What else would you like to know about this person?

_____

Name _____ Date _____

Lion for Mayor!
Mouse for Mayor!

Have you heard the story of the Lion and the Mouse? A mouse wakes up a lion and makes the lion very angry. The mouse begs the lion to let him go. The mouse says the lion might need his help someday.

The lion lets the mouse go, although the lion can't see how such a small creature could ever help him.

Sometime later, the lion is caught in a hunter's net. The mouse chews through the net and frees the lion. The lion learns that size doesn't always matter.

Imagine that both the lion and the mouse were running for mayor. Whom would you vote for?

Cast of Characters:

Lion	Giraffe	Hippo
Mouse	Bird	
Elephant	Snake	

Elephant: Today we will hear from two animals. Each wants to be our new mayor. Let's hear what each one has to say. First, let's welcome Lion.

[Everyone claps.]

Lion: I'm often called the King of Beasts. Why not add mayor to that? *(laughs)* Animals, I would be a good mayor. I am big and brave. I am kind. In fact, I just spared the life of a small animal who made me mad. Kindness counts. Vote for Lion for mayor!

Elephant: Thank you, Lion. And now, welcome Mouse.

[Everyone claps.]

Mouse: Are you wondering how such a small animal could be your leader? Ask Lion. When the great lion was stuck in a net, who got him out? It was I, a tiny mouse. I am small but I am brave and smart. That's what you need in a mayor. Vote for Mouse for mayor!

Elephant: Now it's time for the voters to choose.

Snake: I'm not sure which one to vote for. Each one s-s-s-sounds good.

Monkey: L-i-o-n! Lion, Lion, is sure to win!

Giraffe: Put Mouse in the mayor's house! Put

Mouse in the mayor's house!

Hippo: The choice is up to each of us. We have to

think about which one we think would do the better

job. Then vote.

Bird: May the best animal win!

Write About It Whom would you vote for? Tell why.

_____

_____

_____

_____

_____

 # Ways to Earn Money

Talk with children about the ways they get money. Lead children to see that one way to get money is to earn it. People earn money by being paid for jobs that they do. Explain that when a person does a job, there is a trade. One person gets a job done, and the other person gets money in return. Remind children that another way they may get money is by someone giving them money as a gift.

Read aloud the following introduction:

> Do you think that you can earn money? You may be able to do some jobs and get paid for your work. Then you can save the money or spend it for something you want.
>
> What kinds of jobs can you do?
>
> Look at the list of jobs on the page. Circle jobs that you think you would like to do. Add other jobs that you think of.
>
> For each job, figure out how much money you might earn.

Read the chart on page 61 with children. Discuss reasonable amounts that they might be paid for each job. Then have partners work together to brainstorm additional jobs that they might do, and add them to the chart along with the fees they would charge. Invite children to share the jobs they added to their charts.

Bringing Social Studies Alive
60
Use with *School and Family*

Name _____ Date _____

 # Ways to Earn Money

Here are some jobs that you might be able to do
to earn money. If you would like to do the jobs
listed, circle them. Add to the chart other jobs.
List how much you think you would
be paid.

Job	Pay
walking a neighbor's dog	$1 per week
putting away the trash can	25¢ per week
setting the table for dinner	10¢ per day

Managing Money

Use a chart with pictures of coins and bills to review currency names and amounts for pennies, nickels, dimes, quarters, and dollars.

Give each child play money. Ask children to identify the penny, nickel, dime, quarter, and dollar. Ask how much each is worth.

Then ask children to count out five of each type of currency and tell the amount.

Explain to children that it is important to know the value of coins and bills when buying goods and services. Guide children in selecting the correct coins to pay for something. Read the following traditional rhyme to children.

> I asked my mother
>
> For fifteen cents
>
> To see the elephant
>
> Jump over the fence.
>
> He jumped so high
>
> That he touched the sky
>
> And never came back
>
> 'til the Fourth of July!

Ask children to use their play money to show different combinations of coins that can make up fifteen cents. Circulate and check children's work. Discuss the various combinations.

Have children complete page 63. Ask them to cut out the coins. Tell them to glue a combination of coins to show how they might pay. Point out that there are several different combinations of coins to equal 25 cents, but that they only have to show one. Explain that children will not use all the coin cutouts provided.

 **Managing Money**

Read the rhyme. Cut out the coins. Use different combinations to show different ways to pay.

I asked my mother

For twenty-five cents more

To see the elephant

Jump over the door.

He jumped so low

He stubbed his toe

And that was the end

Of the elephant show!

Show 25¢

Use with *School and Family*

Spending Money

Explain to children that families do not have enough money to buy all the things they want. Families must make choices.

Read the following scenario to children:

> The Smith family had a family meeting to make a list of things they wanted to buy. The things they came up with were a new microwave oven, a DVD player, and a printer for the computer. Their old microwave can't be fixed. They've never had a DVD player. The printer they have now is very slow and doesn't print in color. The family has only enough money to buy one of the items.

Lead children in a discussion about the scenario. Ask the following questions:

- What does the family want to buy?
- Why don't they get all three things?
- How should the family decide which thing to buy?

Organize children into small groups. Have children work together to complete the chart on the following page as they work through the process of making a choice.

Name _____ Date _____

 **Spending Money**

Write a reason why each item is a good choice.

Item	Why it's a good choice
Microwave oven	
DVD player	
Printer	

What choice is the best choice for the family?
Why?

_____

_____

Name _____ Date _____

 **Making Choices**

Look at the amount of money at the beginning
of the row. Circle the picture that shows what
you would buy. Tell why.

I have.	I want. Circle one.	Why?
50¢		_____ _____ _____
30¢		_____ _____ _____
25¢		_____ _____ _____

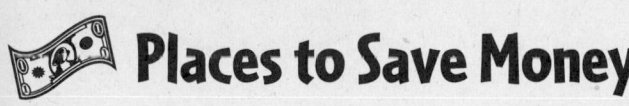

Places to Save Money

Explain to children that they do not have to spend all the money they receive at one time. They can save their money. When you save money, you keep it to spend at a later time. Over time, you can add more money to that amount and end up with a greater amount.

Ask children to brainstorm a list of things that people save money to buy.

Then read aloud the following introduction.

Suppose that a family member gives you $50! You decide that you want to save the money rather than spend it.

How will you save the money?

Organize children into groups. Have groups work together to complete the chart on the following page and make a decision about the best way to save the money.

Use with *School and Family*

Name _____ Date _____

Places to Save Money

Here are some places to save money. Fill in the
chart. Answer the questions.

Places to Save	Why is this a good place?	Why is this not a good place?
Put in drawer.		
Give to parent.		
Put in piggy bank.		
Take to a bank.		

Where would you save money? Why?

_____

 # Saving Money

Read the saying below. With a partner, talk about what you think the saying means. Make a poster about saving money.

Save some money for a rainy day.

To make the poster:

1. Cut out the saying.

2. Paste it on drawing paper.

3. Draw a picture that shows how you can save money.

4. Write a sentence to go with your picture.

5. Share your poster with your partner.

Name _____ Date _____

20 ____ ____

Sunday	Monday	Tuesday	Wednesday	Thursday	Friday	Saturday

Use with *School and Family*

January Activities

Complete the Calendar Have children write the name of the month and fill in the numerals for the year and the days. List these special days on the board and discuss them with children: New Year's Day (January 1); Martin Luther King, Jr., Day (third Monday); National Handwriting Day (January 23); National Puzzle Day (January 29). Then have children draw symbols or write words in the spaces for these and other important January days to remember.

Write a Letter Share with children that January 8–14 is designated as Universal Letter-Writing Week so that people all over the world can begin the new year by sending letters to friends and people in faraway places. Invite children to write a letter to a family member or friend.

Clean It Up! Explain to children that the second Monday in January is National Clean Off Your Desk Day. Provide children with paper towels to use to clean their desks.

February Activities

Complete the Calendar Have children write the name of the month and fill in the numerals for the year and the days. List these special days on the board and discuss them with children: Groundhog Day (February 2); Valentine's Day (February 14); Presidents' Day (third Monday). Then have children draw symbols or write words in the spaces for these and other important February days to remember.

Celebrate Black History Explain that February is Black History Month. To help celebrate, each day play music by an African American performer or composer. In addition, read a poem by an African American or have children participate in a choral reading.

Feed the Birds Share with children that February is National Bird Feeding Month because this winter month in some places is usually a difficult time for birds to find food. Create bird feeders by drizzling honey on pine cones or empty tissue rolls and rolling them in birdseed. Attach yarn so that children can hang the feeder at home or at school.

March Activities

Complete the Calendar Have children write the name of the month and fill in the numerals for the year and the days. List these special days on the board and discuss them with children: Dr. Seuss Day (March 2); St. Patrick's Day (March 17); Make Up Your Own Holiday Day (March 26). Then have children draw symbols or write words in the spaces for these and other important March days to remember.

Read the Newspaper Explain to children that the first week in March is Newspaper in Education Week. Bring in a newspaper and use it for geography practice. Read aloud an article and call attention to the area mentioned, such as the country, state, city, or neighborhood, and help children locate it on a map.

Sing the National Anthem Share with children that March 3 is National Anthem Day. Listen to a variety of musical recordings of the song. Invite children to sing "The Star-Spangled Banner" and draw a picture to illustrate it.

April Activities

Complete the Calendar Have children write the name of the month and fill in the numerals for the year and the days. List these special days on the board and discuss them with children: April Fool's Day (April 1); Earth Day (April 22); National Playground Safety Day (last Thursday); Arbor Day (last Friday). Then have children draw symbols or write words in the spaces for these and other important April days to remember.

Save Money Share with children that April 22 is National Teach Children to Save Day. Invite children to make a piggy bank from a clean milk jug or other container. Discuss reasons to save money. Suggest they talk to their family about opening a bank account.

Celebrate Trees The last Friday in April is Arbor Day. Discuss the meaning of the word *arbor*. Read books featuring trees. If possible, plant a tree in a container in the classroom, such as a Norfolk Island pine. Lead children in creating artwork based on trees, such as a bark rubbing of a tree on the school grounds or making leaf prints.

Bringing Social Studies Alive
72
Use with *School and Family*

May Activities

Complete the Calendar Have children write the name of the month and fill in the numerals for the year and the days. List these special days on the board and discuss them with children: School Principals' Day (May 1); National Teacher's Day (May 4); Mother's Day (second Sunday); Memorial Day (last Monday). Then have children draw symbols or write words in the spaces for these and other important May days to remember.

Track Sports and Fitness Activities Share with children that May is National Physical Fitness and Sports Month. Brainstorm a variety of sports and fitness activities. Encourage children to try at least three new activities during the month. Encourage children to use their calendars to record their daily physical activity.

Show Police Appreciation Tell children that the week of May that includes the 15th is always Police Appreciation Week. Have children make appreciation cards for local officers. Mail the cards to a local police station.

June Activities

Complete the Calendar Have children write the name of the month and fill in the numerals for the year and the days. List these special days on the board and discuss them with children: Flag Day (June 14); Father's Day (third Sunday); summer begins (June 21 or 22). Then have children draw symbols or write words in the spaces for these and other important June days to remember.

Chart Dairy Favorites Share with children that June is Dairy Month. Discuss various dairy products. Invite children to select two favorites, and graph the results.

Make a Flag Display Explain that Flag Day is a day to honor the flag of our country. If possible, use crepe paper and foam cups to weave a flag display in a chain link fence on the school grounds. Alternatively, invite children to bring in photos of flags, flag stickers, computer printouts of the flag, or flag drawings to create a classroom display. Invite children to participate in the Pause for the Pledge—people all across the nation recite the pledge at 7 P.M. EDT.

Use with *School and Family*

July Activities

Complete the Calendar Have children write the name of the month and fill in the numerals for the year and the days. List these special days on the board and discuss them with children: Independence Day (July 4); first astronauts land on moon (July 20, 1969); National Ice Cream Day (third Sunday). Then have children draw symbols or write words in the spaces for these and other important July days to remember.

Learn About American Symbols Share with children images of Uncle Sam, and explain that the images are symbols of America. Point out that the beginning letters *U.S.* are the same as our country's name. Invite children to draw their own picture of Uncle Sam. Display the pictures around the classroom. You may want to review the symbols in the pupil edition Unit 5, Lesson 5.

Spin a Story Tell children that storytelling festivals are held throughout the country in July. Invite children to tell stories in small groups about historical events, such as Washington crossing the Delaware or Betsy Ross sewing the flag.

August Activities

Complete the Calendar Have children write the name of the month and fill in the numerals for the year and the days. List these special days on the board and discuss them with children: Columbus sets sail for Asia (August 3, 1492); National Aviation Day (August 19, birthday of Orville Wright). Then have children draw symbols or write words in the spaces for these and other important August days to remember.

Invent It! Share with children that August is National Inventors' Month. Work with children through the invention process by identifying a classroom problem and brainstorming an invention to solve the problem. Have children draw a diagram of the invention.

Reach Out and Learn Tell children that August 12 is United Nations International Youth Day. Explain that the United Nations is a group of people from many countries who work for world peace and the well-being of all people. Invite children to use nonfiction materials to learn about children in other countries.

Use with *School and Family*

September Activities

Complete the Calendar Have children write the name of the month and fill in the numerals for the year and the days. List these special days on the board and discuss them with children: Labor Day (first Monday); National Grandparents' Day (first Sunday after Labor Day); Video Games Day (September 12). Then have children draw symbols or write words in the spaces for these and other important September days to remember.

Write a School Success List Share with children that September is National School Success Month. Have them brainstorm a list of things that they and their families can do to help ensure school success.

Show Manners, Please! Share with children that September is Children's Good Manners Month. Ask them to fold a paper into fourths and illustrate four ways that they will use good manners this month.

October Activities

Complete the Calendar Have children write the name of the month and fill in the numerals for the year and the days. List these special days on the board and discuss them with children: Columbus Day (second Monday); National Bring Your Teddy Bear to Work and School Day (October 8); National Grouch Day (October 15); Halloween (October 31). Then have children draw symbols or write words in the spaces for these and other important October days to remember.

Sing a Fire Prevention Song Share with children that Fire Prevention Week is the first or second week of October. Review fire safety information. Help children use this information to compose a song to a familiar tune, such as "Three Blind Mice" or "Twinkle, Twinkle Little Star."

Pledge to Bus Safety Explain that National School Bus Safety Week is the third week of October. Have children generate a list of school bus safety rules. Ask them to write a pledge that tells how they promise to stay safe on school buses.

November Activities

Complete the Calendar Have children write the name of the month and fill in the numerals for the year and the days. List these special days on the board and discuss them with children: Sandwich Day (November 3); Veterans' Day (November 11); What Do You Love About America? Day (fourth Wednesday); Thanksgiving Day (fourth Thursday); Ramadan (dates vary). Then have children draw symbols or write words in the spaces for these and other important November days to remember.

Celebrate Children's Books Explain to children that the week before Thanksgiving is National Children's Book Week. Have children choose their favorite book and tell about it.

Say Hello! Share with children that World Hello Day can be celebrated on November 21. Tell children to celebrate the day by greeting ten students in school. People in over 180 countries take part in this event to encourage peace through personal communication.

December Activities

Complete the Calendar Have children write the name of the month and fill in the numerals for the year and the days. List these special days on the board and discuss them with children: Hanukkah (dates vary); Christmas (December 25); first day of Kwanzaa, an African American holiday (December 26); New Year's Eve, December 31. Then have children draw symbols or write words in the spaces for these and other important December days to remember.

Dribble and Shoot December 1 is the anniversary of the creation of the game of basketball. Point out that it was created by a physical education teacher as an indoor sport for the winter months. Engage children in practicing dribbling and shooting a basketball.

Broadcast It Explain that the second Sunday in December is International Children's Day of Broadcasting. Broadcasters around the world create special programs to celebrate children. Have small groups of children work together to present a mini-broadcast about what's happening in your classroom or school.

Answer Key

Unit 1

Page 4: Draw a Map

Possible responses: checkout counter, book-shelves, tables, chairs.

Children's map of the library should reflect an understanding of a view from above.

Page 5: Use a Map Key

1. swing   3. slide
2. tree

Children should also draw a bench in the map, add a bench symbol to the map key, and write the word *bench.*

Unit 2

Page 16: The Bear Went Over the Landforms Game

Children should be able to identify the land-forms and bodies of water—ocean, mountain, plain, river, and lake—on the map.

Page 22: Prop Talk Plan

Possible answers:

Bag with tree: pencil, paper, wooden toy, book

Bag with river: drinking water, fish

Bag with a hole in the ground: gold, silver, kitchen silverware, tools

Bag with a tomato plant: salad, spaghetti sauce, tomato juice, tomato soup

Unit 3

Page 28: Goods and Services Map

Goods: pet shop, furniture store Services: hair cuts, post office, dentist, car repair, city library

Unit 4

Page 42: Personal History Timeline

Children's timeline should reflect appropriate events for the ages.

Unit 5

Page 53: Laws and Signs

Check that these signs are in the correct places: four stop signs near each corner; a DO NOT ENTER sign on Plum street next to the school's driveway; a NO PARKING sign on Plum street across from the schools' driveway; a SCHOOL ZONE sign across from the school on Third Avenue.

Page 56: Meet a Leader or Hero

Answers will vary, but should reflect accurate answers and good questions about their chosen leader or hero.

Page 61: Ways to Earn Money

Circled jobs will vary. The list of other jobs and pay will vary, but should reflect reasonable jobs and pay for children.

Page 63: Managing Money

Children should show two different combina-tions of coins that equal 25¢. Example: Five nickles; two dimes and one nickle.

Page 65: Spending Money

Children's answers for why each item is a good choice or not a good choice should be reason-able ones based on decision-making criteria.

Page 66: Making Choices

Answers will vary. Children should be able to support the choices they make.

Page 68: Places to Save Money

Answers will vary. Children should conclude that giving money to a parent or taking it to a bank would keep their money safe.